INTERVENTION

CONFRONTING A LOVED ONE WHO USES DRUGS

Confronting someone about his or her drug use is never easy.

THE DRUG ABUSE PREVENTION LIBRARY

INTERVENTION
CONFRONTING A LOVED ONE WHO USES DRUGS

Craig Konieczko

The Rosen Publishing Group, Inc.
New York

Published in 2000 by The Rosen Publishing Group, Inc.
29 East 21st Street, New York, NY 10010

Copyright © 2000 by The Rosen Publishing Group, Inc.

First Edition

Library of Congress Cataloging-in-Publication Data

Konieczko, Craig
    Intervention / Craig Konieczko.
      p. cm. — (The drug abuse prevention library)
    Includes bibliographical references and index.
    Summary: Discusses strategies that friends and family members may use to make a teen face up to his or her addiction and get support to overcome it.
    ISBN 0-8239-3156-0 (lib. bdg.)
    1. Alcoholics—Rehabilitation—Juvenile literature. 2. Narcotic addicts—Rehabilitation—Juvenile literature. 3. Crisis Intervention (Mental health services)—Juvenile literature. [1. Alcoholics—Rehabilitation. 2. Narcotic addicts—Rehabilitation. 3. Crisis Intervention (Mental health services).] I. Title. II. Series.
    RC564.3 .K66 2000
    362.29'18—dc21
                                           99-052411
                                             CIP
                                           AC

Manufactured in the United States of America

Contents

Introduction

Heat rises off the basketball court. Antonio is ready to play. There is only one problem: Enrique is nowhere to be found.

Much later in the afternoon, Enrique arrives with a brown paper bag. Inside is an open bottle of malt liquor. "All right, let's go," he shouts, as he steals the ball and shoots.

But Antonio backs away and doesn't try to defend the hoop. "Sorry, you're too late. And besides, I don't want to play with you when you're drunk. You're too slow." He grabs his towel, wipes his face, and sits down.

Antonio decided that enough is enough. Even though he loves to shoot hoops, he does not want to play with a friend who is drinking.

Like Antonio, you may know someone—probably a friend or a relative—who needs help to stop using alcohol or other drugs. This person may even be seriously addicted. Helping him or her is not something you can do alone, but don't worry. There are family members, friends, and trained counselors who will work with you. Maybe your friend has lived with an addiction for a while. Maybe you have lived with this addiction, too. Your friend is close to you, but when this person uses a drug, he or she is difficult to deal with. There are probably many times that your friend has disappointed and hurt you.

This book will help you to understand what an intervention is, and it will prepare you for participation in an intervention. Intervention means "stepping in and putting a stop or halt to something." In terms of addiction, it means making an addicted person face reality. The process is a series of steps toward a destination, or many single actions toward a goal. As you read this book, you will come to understand the many steps of the intervention process.

You will also learn about the many different types of interventions. Sometimes an

8

intervention is one-on-one. Others require weeks of group meetings and preparation. This book explains how to get ready for either type of intervention. This book is not intended for use as a resource for organizing and leading an intervention, but it will show you what your role is. You will learn how an intervention can help your addicted loved one and how it can help you and other family members, too. This is true even if this person does not accept help right away.

As you begin to learn about interventions, you will have many questions and concerns. You may have a hard time imagining a day when you and your family will have to speak frankly to someone with an addiction. You may not even believe that other family members or friends have been hurt like you. And you may feel that you are the only person who thinks that there is a serious problem. This book will help prepare you to talk to your addicted friend or family member in a way that can only help everyone involved.

One last note: It is important to remember that you are not at fault. You didn't cause the problem, and the outcome of the intervention is not your responsibility. However, by reading this book, you show that you care about yourself as well as the person with an addiction. You want to be ready to help yourself as much as you want to help your friend, parent, sibling, or relative.

Prior to an intervention, many confrontations about a loved one's substance abuse habits have usually taken place.

CHAPTER 1

Why Does Your Loved One Need Help?

Last night Laura met up with her new boyfriend at his house. They took his car across town and smoked a joint, and then drank a beer or two. When she got home her mom was asleep, so she thought that she could go to bed unnoticed.

But today when Laura got home after school, her mom was very angry. "You were supposed to come to my cooking class last night. Where were you? And what has gotten into you lately? You are not the daughter I know!"

"I was studying late with Cedric. And anyway, you can't tell me where to go and what to do," said Laura, storming out of the room.

Her mom is not yet sure if Laura has been using drugs of any kind. She suspects that her daughter might be. But what can her mom do if Laura reacts so negatively when challenged?

People turn to drugs for many reasons, such as depression.

Drugs, such as alcohol and marijuana, are substances that people use to feel high. Some people use these and other drugs to help them handle stress, depression, anger, helplessness, and fear. These are feelings that people do not enjoy, but they are part of life. Others turn to drugs so that they can rebel or experiment. All people have days when they are tired, angry, over-worked, or when they feel very much alone. Most people relieve these feelings through proper outlets—sports, hobbies, or just getting enough sleep. But some-times people feel, for whatever reason, that they just cannot get away from their prob-lems and the stresses they create. In our society drugs are waiting for anyone who wants to turn to them. Their pull is powerful. People will risk arrest and even death to obtain illegal drugs.

What Is Addiction?

Addiction is the physical or psychological need to use a chemical substance again and again. The body is addicted when it requires a chemical substance to function normally. How does someone get to this stage? When a person first tries a drug, he or she experiences a high. If the person tries the drug repeatedly, soon the body adapts to that substance. The body develops a tolerance for the drug, requiring more and more of it to produce the same good feeling. If the drug is not available, a person experiences painful withdrawal symptoms. Eventually a person needs the drug just to feel normal. This is a later stage of addiction. Because of the changes that occur in the body as it learns to handle a chemical substance, addiction is considered an illness.

Just like any other illness, addiction has symptoms. These include denial that there is a problem, at the very same time that the need to find and use the drug becomes more urgent. These symptoms create problems for families and draw them into the

14

sickness. In the earlier example, Laura denied her problems when her mother reached out to her. Then her mother became confused and worried. In the end her mom was only more unsure about what to do. If Laura is addicted to drugs and alcohol, the symptoms will prevent her from realizing that she is doing harm to herself and her mom.

People who are addicted usually don't realize that they cause a tremendous amount of pain for others and themselves. The behavior of an addicted person blunts his or her awareness of the suffering inflicted on others. Friends and relatives are not to be blamed for this behavior, but they must take firm action if they want to protect themselves from further abuse, as well as help the addict. The addicted person is responsible for his or her own recovery, but those around this person may have to give the addict a hard but supportive push in the right direction. This is what intervention is all about.

The Symptoms of Addiction

When a person is addicted, his or her body needs more and more of a drug just to feel normal. Becoming high is harder because the body becomes more and more tolerant of the drug and will accept a certain amount of the drug without feeling its effects.

But no matter how tolerant your addicted friend or family member may be, there are certain symptoms that a person will inevitably show during and after a high. These symptoms make everyone's life especially difficult because they cause the addicted person to forget real events and to deny reality. If your loved one hurt you last night, he or she may not even remember what happened. Side effects such as blackouts lead to denial, which your intervention will try to overcome.

Chloe and Jim sat at the kitchen table of the small two-room apartment they rent together. Jim put down his glass as Chloe said, "C'mon Jim, tell me what's bothering you! You're acting strange, and I want to know what's going on."

"All right, then. What I have to tell you is very, very hard for me, but I've got to say it. I'm moving out this afternoon. I can't stand the way you have been shooting heroin and the way it makes you act. You're so withdrawn and out of it. Last night I tried to tell you about my art exhibit, and you were so stoned you didn't

Drug addiction destroys relationships.

even know who I was. Last Wednesday I found you walking around alone on the roof of the building. You were going way too close to the edge! You can't control yourself, and I can't have a relationship with you."

Chloe slammed her fork and knife down on the table, spilling rice and vegetables off her plate. "How can you say that? I wasn't even home last night until after you fell asleep. I don't remember seeing you at all. You make up this stuff because you don't love me and you just want an excuse to leave me in this dump. You're a coward with no good reason to walk out on me. Last night I wasn't even high!"

Jim hated to be spoken to this way, but it

was not the first time. He felt a wave of anxiety

come over him. "Maybe I was wrong . . . Maybe she was just really tired last night," he thought. In truth, Chloe cannot remember a word of what Jim said the night before about his artwork.

Chloe doesn't remember what really happened the night before because she suffered a blackout as a result of her use of heroin. A blackout occurs when a person's mind completely erases the memory of what happened when he or she was high. These blackouts can last anywhere from a few seconds to several days. During a blackout, an addicted person functions, but afterward he or she cannot remember a single thing that occurred.

Another problem faced by people who are abusing or addicted to drugs and alcohol is known as euphoric recall. The addicted person possesses the ability to remember the positive feeling of the drug high but does not remember any negative actions.

Rob and his buddies like to get drunk before school dances and parties. They have been drinking before school events for several months. Rob feels like the "king of the school," as he puts it, when he arrives late after some drinking.

18

One Friday evening he went to a dance with a couple of friends. They had been drinking hard liquor, so they used strong breath mints to cover the smell. The pounding beat of the loud music went right through Rob's body, and he started to dance harder and harder. A little while later he moved to the back of the gymnasium where some students had installed a sculpture exhibit.

Rob didn't see it, or maybe he just couldn't control himself. He didn't stop as his body slammed into a delicate cardboard sculpture. The artwork was ruined, but no one saw him destroy it. He quickly walked to the other side of the gym and found his friends.

Since no one will ever be able to accuse Rob of destroying another student's artwork, he will not have to deal with the consequences of this episode. The next day, when he thinks about what he did the night before, he might recall only how much energy he felt he had. He could have danced all night! The fact that he did something that cost another person so much lost time and satisfaction does not dawn on him at all. His euphoric recall allows him to remember only the positive feelings he experienced as a result of his drinking.

How Does Your Loved One's Addiction Affect You?

Rob's lack of physical control over his body, caused by his drinking, had a real consequence for a classmate. Chloe's blackout had an even greater psychological consequence for her boyfriend, Jim, who feels frustrated when he can no longer be certain what had really gone on in the apartment only twenty-four hours earlier.

Blackouts affect the people around the addicted person because they support that person's denial of reality. If the person suffering from a blackout mistreats family members, it is more difficult to confront that person. He or she will not remember a single word of a hateful conversation or any of the crazy things he or she did while high. What can a concerned loved one like Jim do when his girlfriend suffers from such severe denial?

Because his one-on-one intervention met with such strong resistance from Chloe, Jim might begin to feel hopeless. He might begin to support Chloe's explanations for her drug use out of the hope that he might be wrong. She may try to tell him that she might not use drugs if he wasn't away from home all the time. She is trying to blame him

20 | for her behavior. If Jim goes along with this reasoning, he enables Chloe. To enable someone is to help that person to continue to use drugs. Jim may feel guilty when he does realize what is happening, but he does not know how to break this cycle.

Jim falls into another trap when he confronts his girlfriend about her use of heroin. When he tells her that he is moving out today, he blames and threatens Chloe. If he does not follow through with his threat, Chloe will learn that future threats will not have consequences either. Jim will feel even more helpless than before. He even questions his own perception of what is happening around him.

Intervention Is the Next Step

When your loved one has become addicted, he or she has lost control of his or her behavior and has also lost touch with reality. Family members, coworkers, and friends may first try confrontation and blame. Then they themselves deny that the problem exists and even enable their addicted loved one to continue self-destructive behavior. Such a pattern can go on for years. The loved one can become very sick and even die before anyone ever realizes that the addicted person has hit bottom. Codependency is a term for the behavior of family or friends that allows an addicted person to continue to use drugs. Family members become codependent because they are afraid to hurt or anger their addicted loved one.

Now that you understand the way addiction works, you can better understand why you are not to blame, even if you have enabled your loved one to continue using drugs or alcohol. You can now learn about how you can participate in an intervention that will show your addicted loved one a new reality while ending the enabling, denial, and guilt that plague your relationship with this person.

CHAPTER 2

What Is an Intervention?

If you are reading this book because you are going to take part in an intervention, then someone has probably already taken the first step of contacting an intervention counselor. There are many resources listed at the end of this book where you can get information about intervention counseling. In a family group intervention, a counselor brings the family members and friends of the addicted person together to educate and train them. This takes place during several sessions before the actual meeting with the person who needs help. You and your intervention group may have already begun your meetings, or perhaps you are

Calling a hotline can be the first step toward an intervention.

going to begin soon. Even if you are not participating in an intervention anytime soon, this book will help you understand what happens.

As you read in the last chapter, addiction makes communication very difficult. There are reasons, both physical and psychological, that explain why your loved one denies, or pretends, in order to resist facing reality. Also, your family or group of friends may enable, or help, the addicted person to continue to use a chemical substance. You and the rest of your group initially come to the intervention process with anger and a sense of frustration and hopelessness. You may also come with a set of conditioned behaviors

24 that don't really help anyone. Conditioned behaviors are learned habitual actions that a person uses in order to cope with, or get through, difficult situations. For example, imagine trying to reason with an addicted friend. You tell him to stop using a drug because you have seen another person die after abusing the same substance. But your friend becomes angry with you. To avoid placing your friendship at risk, you learn to stop bringing up this topic.

The Preparation

Obstacles such as enabling and denial can make intervention very difficult. This is why preparation is so important. Whether you plan to intervene alone (one-on-one) or with a trained team (group intervention), you will need to prepare carefully, to learn techniques that will help you to overcome the addicted person's evasions and denial. This time you are not going to enable the addicted person to continue his or her behavior by avoiding the subject or by accepting that person's version of events.

One-on-One Interventions

After her first two years in high school, Janet succeeded in earning a place with the school's peer counseling group. She began volunteering during weekends to listen to anonymous calls on her community's youth crisis hotline. She had trained for many hours in order to become certified to handle calls on her own, but on her first day she was still nervous. Of course, there was a professional social worker on staff at the call center. He could help out and take over if a situation went beyond Janet's level of expertise.

Janet handled a few calls about romantic relationships and stress over schoolwork. But her next call, from someone named Chris, was more difficult.

"Last night my sister came home in a police car. She smokes pot and does some other drugs, but last night she was totally strung out. They found her hanging out in a parking lot downtown real late. I think she was with this older guy who gets drugs for her, but he must have left before she got picked up. Now my parents have her. My dad just thanked the cops and took her inside. Now here's the worst part. After the cops left, my dad sat her down and screamed at her. Just yelled and yelled for an hour about how she was wasting her life away with that guy. He didn't even really talk about drugs. It was terrible, and she was out of it. She didn't even hear most of what he said, I'm sure."

25

26   *Janet listened supportively. She knew that the father didn't help matters with his unplanned "intervention."*

Chris did not use drugs like his older sister. He recognized that his sister has a problem with drug use. And he also saw that his father's response, although realistic and maybe even expected, was not helpful. Chris did not know how to help his sister. Once he tried to talk to his father about her problem, but his dad did not want to talk about it. Chris called the hotline as a first step toward seeking the counseling that could lead to an intervention. But before this intervention could occur, some things would have to change.

After his sister's crisis, Chris's dad tried to reason with her, but he blamed her and yelled at her. The father had not yet realized that his reaction was in fact pushing his daughter away from a helpful intervention. Chris, on the other hand, realized that there is a better way.

Even most one-on-one interventions often involve a third party—a counselor, a social worker, a member of a religious group, or a trained interventionist. This third party is sometimes necessary because family members, like Chris's father, must overcome

their own enabling behavior in order to help.
Sometimes family members are so caught up in the patterns of addiction that they cannot lead effectively. Family members who have spent years covering up for their addicted loved one do not always readily accept the ground rules of a formal intervention. Overcoming these obstacles sometimes requires training plus the perspective of an outsider.

After the first season of high school junior varsity tennis, coaches noticed that Arielle was a rising star. She made her ground strokes with a finesse and ease that not many others could duplicate. When Arielle's mom made her attend tennis camp away from home that summer, she started to feel more pressure than she could handle.

Later that summer she began to drink beer with friends, and she started to cut practices. When she returned to the team in the fall, she had lost her focus. She no longer played well, and the coaches cut her from the team because of her absences. But she did not care. She told her mom that she had new interests. She wanted to spend more time with new friends who liked to party.

Arielle's boyfriend, Josh, couldn't believe that she had given up on tennis. He knew of her drinking but didn't yet understand that it

A school counselor can intervene in an emergency situation.

had become a problem. Still, he tried to bring it up to her several times. She never wanted to talk about it. Once she became very angry and did not speak to him for three days.

One day after school, Josh went to see a teacher about a test he had almost failed. "What's wrong, Josh? You just don't seem to be having any fun," asked Mr. Jackson. Josh said that he was having some "girlfriend problems" but nothing more. When Mr. Jackson asked him more about it, Josh mentioned that Arielle was drinking. Mr. Jackson suggested that seeing a school counselor might help her out. Josh agreed and made an appointment. After speaking together for a few minutes, the counselor decided to meet with Arielle to talk about these recent changes in her life. The counselor asked Josh to

help him get ready for this intervention. He asked
Josh about what he had observed and how
Arielle's drinking had affected him.

A school counselor may intervene right away, after he or she is notified that a student has been drinking or has a problem with drugs. Of course, each situation is handled differently, but the counselor is generally obligated by law to contact parents. He may try to have the student discuss the situation first.

Group Interventions

If the addicted person is a parent or an older friend or relative, then the intervention will probably involve more planning at first. Very often a trained counselor or interventionist will lead this training.

Jay's mother, Janice, was supposed to pick him up after his Saturday computer class at one o'clock. When she arrived at five minutes past two she looked tired. She had been using her tranquilizer pills. While driving home with Jay, she swerved the car over the double yellow line and back several times, making the rest of the ride home very scary. Luckily there wasn't too much traffic.

Two days later Janice couldn't get up to go to work on Monday morning. Jay's father, Jorge, had to call her office and report her

It is extremely difficult and painful to watch a loved one's self-destructive behavior.

sick, but really she had had too much to drink the previous night.

When Jay saw his mother as he was getting ready for school that morning, he was scared. She looked hollow inside. Her eyes were sunken and did not shine like they used to. She could barely move without tripping and shaking. Jay went to school feeling that he had to do the best he could. "If I get any bad grades, it will make it even harder for her," he thought during his first class.

That afternoon Carla, Jay's aunt, came over to visit. Even though Jorge told her that Janice was sick, Carla knew better. During the visit Carla could not believe how terrible her sister looked—her eyes, her skin, the shaking fingers. That day Carla realized how bad

things had become, and she was no longer
willing to just sit by and watch her sister get
sicker and sicker.

In this typical addiction scenario, Janice's substance abuse places a lot of pressure on her family. Fortunately, Carla, who does not live in the same household, can help. After her Monday afternoon visit, she made an appointment with a counselor who will begin the intervention process. Carla then called Jorge and asked him to bring Jay to the first meeting.

Jay knows almost everyone in the counselor's office: his dad; Janice's brother Derek; Carla; his eleven-year-old sister, Harriet; and even his mom's coworker and friend, Jeannie. There is only one person he does not know: the counselor. His name is Steve, and he starts the meeting. "You are all here because you care about Janice very deeply. Let's start by having each of you tell us your favorite thing about her."

At the first meeting of the intervention group, the counselor does a lot of the talking and asks a lot of questions. He or she tries to determine if each person involved will make an effective member of the intervention team. Sometimes family members are afraid to participate. They

32 might say, "Janice will be angry at me" or "I'm not the kind of person who can open up like this." However, these people can overcome their fears. Other family members may be angry that they have been invited, or they are certain that interventions cannot work. The counselor will recommend to the group leader who should and should not participate.

Who should join this group? One of the most important things to remember about intervention is that it is not a time to accuse or blame your addicted loved one. People who are likely to do this should not participate. Other people refuse to accept that addiction is an illness. They consider those who are addicted to be individuals with a weakness in dealing with life's problems. If these people are not willing to learn about and accept a different viewpoint, they will not make good team members. These people are not bad; they simply have a different opinion. The counselor knows that the group needs to act fast and must communicate with the addicted person without anger and blame. There may not be time to educate these people so that they can join the group.

Janice's brother Derek believes that people with drinking problems are weak and that they are to blame for their condition. **33** He declines to attend after the first meeting, although he says that he hopes it all works out for the best. This is an instance when the presence of a counselor can help to reduce the anger between family members that could destroy the intervention process.

Carla, Janice's sister, brought the group together. Since she does not live with the addicted loved one every day, she has more perspective on how Janice's addictions affect those close to her. Carla has tried confrontation and one-on-one intervention in the past. But she has seen Janice relapse again. A relapse is when a drug user returns to drug use after a period of not using. This time Carla wants to help and make it work.

Janice's coworker and friend, Jeannie, has known her for five years. Janice's problems have entered the workplace, and Jeannie has had to cover for her friend several times. The counselor believes that Jeannie will be very important during the intervention. This is because Jeannie is about the same age as Janice, and she is not a family member. Sometimes hearing about a problem from someone who is outside of your family is even more convincing.

Jorge, Janice's husband, knows intimately how his wife suffers from her illness.

34 He is sensitive to the ways her problem has hurt the entire family, and he is keenly aware of every instance in which she has let down someone in the family. Nevertheless, he has spent many years making excuses for his wife and protecting their children. He must overcome this denial. Jay will join the group, along with his sister, Harriet.

How Much Planning Is Needed for an Intervention?

If a school counselor discovers that a student is addicted to drugs, he may choose to intervene right away. In a position of official responsibility, this person will contact parents and teachers as he reaches out to the troubled student. This type of intervention does not involve convincing a young person to go for treatment. By law, parents must be notified, and the parent or guardian can send his or her addicted child for inpatient treatment.

One-on-one interventions without a counselor are often unplanned. Friends who learn as much as they can about addiction and its treatment are more likely to be successful with these unplanned interventions. But there is no required or predetermined preparation time for this kind of intervention.

Only group interventions involve a very structured process. This type of intervention, whether the addicted person is young or old, requires the commitment and training of participants. This takes several weeks, although it is usually different for each family or group. In most cases, a group meet once per week for four or five weeks before intervention day. Here is an example of the preparation schedule:

First meeting: (Monday, June 2, 5 to 7 PM) The counselor welcomes the prospective participants. He or she asks many questions about the addicted loved one and asks about each participant's views on substance abuse and addiction. The counselor explains each step of the intervention and about what is likely to happen on the day of the intervention. Those who wish to participate commit to the entire process. Each person's homework assignment is to write a list of the best qualities of the addicted loved one.

Second meeting: (Tuesday, June 10, 6 to 9 PM) The counselor teaches everyone about addiction: symptoms, denial, and the role that each person in the room plays. Each person thinks about how he or she has enabled the addicted loved one to

36 | continue the addictive behavior, or about how he or she has withheld information from someone who might have helped. Each person's homework assignment is to write down a true story describing an incident in which he or she covered up the addicted person's behavior.

Third meeting: (Monday, June 16, 5 to 7 PM) Group members learn about different ways to handle their loved one's symptoms and behaviors. They learn about tough love, which is the practice of letting an addicted person face the consequences of his or her negative actions. Participants become less judgmental about addiction and about their own enabling behaviors. The homework assignment is to consider a real situation from their lives when they enabled their addicted loved one, and to answer the question, "What else could I have done?"

Fourth meeting: (Wednesday, June 25, 7 to 9 PM) The group answers the question, "What do we want to happen?" Often the answer is to get the addicted person into a treatment program. The group tries to come up with all the possible questions and excuses that their addicted loved one may have. The counselor introduces role-playing.

At a first meeting, the counselor will explain what an intervention is and assess each participant's relationship with the troubled loved one.

Participants are given homework: writing down how they feel about their loved one and describing his or her best qualities.

In later meetings, participants learn about different ways to handle the symptoms and behaviors of their loved one.

He or she pretends to be the loved one while family members talk about situations that hurt or embarrassed them. The homework is to write a "speech" to be read on intervention day.

Fifth meeting: (Wednesday, July 2, 5 to 7 PM) This will be the last meeting before intervention day. Everyone reads his or her homework. A group leader is chosen, and a speaking order is worked out. All necessary tasks, such as driving and picking up participants, packing a bag for the loved one, arranging time off from work, and providing supervision for children, are assigned. The group agrees on a goal, which might be to bring the loved one to a treatment program immediately after the intervention is over. If the loved one refuses to go along with this goal, the group also agrees to stick with tough love.

The next meeting will be with the addicted person on intervention day.

The Most Important Parts of Preparation

If you join an intervention group, even before the intervention takes place, you should:

- Become an expert about addiction and its symptoms

Before an intervention you must do a lot of preparation.

- Stop yourself from practicing enabling behavior

- Start to talk about your family's problem in a helpful way

- Learn that you're not the only one who is suffering

- Realize that there is hope of recovery in every situation

CHAPTER 3

The Day of the Intervention

It is the day of the intervention. You and your group have done all of your homework, and now you will take action. Your group has left no possible situations unrehearsed and no possible reaction unanticipated. Hoping for the best outcome but prepared for anything, your group will try to get your loved one to agree to enter a treatment program today. But you are also ready to begin practicing tough love if your loved one refuses to accept direct help.

Remember that no two interventions are alike. Each addicted person is at a different stage, and each group is comprised of people with different talents and different prejudices to overcome. You will now have the chance to follow along as the events of a group intervention unfold.

The Intervention

Jay feels a surge of fear mixed with happiness as his mom, Janice, walks into her sister Carla's living room. She looks around and stops. She's confused, and maybe even angry. "What's going on here? I thought I was going to relax with my sister!"

"We will," says Carla. "But there's something else that's more important. Please sit down and please do just one thing for us right now. Just listen to what we have to say." Jay notices how Carla sounds different. Maybe she is nervous, too, he thinks.

"I don't understand you at all. What am I going to listen to?" asks Janice, still confused.

"We're all here because we care so much about you," says Carla. "This is going to be hard for all of us. We're all here to talk about your drinking and the pills you take. But for now all we ask is that you patiently listen to each of us."

"What are my kids doing here? They shouldn't be here right now!" exclaims Janice.

"Everyone needs to be here right now because everyone has something to say about this," says Carla. "Now please, Janice, I need to ask you to listen and say no more for now."

42

"Fine, I'll listen, but I'd rather just relax. It's my day off and I don't feel like doing this!" says Janice, as she stares out the window and focuses on a tree in the front yard.

Janice was expecting this day to be like any other. She may have even expected to have a drink while she visited her sister. Instead, she found her family members and a coworker waiting for her. It is natural for anyone in this situation to be both surprised and upset. Notice how the group members take care not to threaten her. Only the team leader, Carla, has spoken, and only she insists that her sister sit down and listen.

As group leader, Carla will make sure that there are no confrontations and that everyone follows the planned speaking order. She will let Janice respond to each person. But she will not allow unplanned discussion. This is not the time to move away from the planned speaking order.

Carla does not have to remind Jorge, Jay, Harriet, and Jeannie when to get their notes ready. Each person has already rehearsed his or her part. Steve, a substance abuse counselor who is also trained to work with intervention groups, sits quietly in the room. He will not need to participate unless there is a problem that Carla cannot solve.

"Okay, why don't you begin," Carla says to Jay, who takes a deep breath.

"Mom, you're the best," Jay says. "I love you and need you every day. I remember all of the fun things you, Harriet, and I have done together. The best thing I remember is when we took that train trip across the whole country to visit Grandma. But for the past year we haven't been together as much. I have to watch Harriet later and later at night while you're out or sleeping. Last week you didn't even try to stay up with us after you came home from work. I was so scared by the way you looked."

Janice thinks for a moment and says, "Honey, I'm dead tired when I get home from work. Someone's got to bring money home and it sure wasn't your dad last year." Janice glares at Jorge, who was out of work for a few months last year.

"Mom, we know it's not easy," Jay answers. "But there's one other thing you should know about. Remember Saturday night about three months ago when I had a couple of friends over? We were playing music when all of a sudden you came in and yelled at me to turn the music down? We apologized right away, but

44 *then you started yelling at my friend Sean to get out of the house. After you calmed down, I acted like I had no idea what was going on, but everyone knew that you had been drinking. And Sean isn't going to hang out anymore, at least not at our house."*

As Jay reads his notes to his mother, he is careful to read only what he planned to say. He begins with something positive by talking about good times and a specific happy time he remembers. This way he tells his mom how much he loves her. Next he moves on to the more difficult part of his speech. He talks about how he has been hurt, scared, and confused because of her addiction. He does not accuse her. He tells only true stories about the hard times he has faced because of her problem. This is the first story that will help Janice understand how her drinking and pill usage affects her loved ones.

Jeannie speaks next. "Janice, I loved to work with you when you were sober. We used to have fun and help each other through the tough days. But I can't say I feel the same anymore, even though I want things to be back the way they were. Two weeks ago, when the supplies for the trucks weren't ready, I had to go out and buy the stuff with my credit card. That was

At first, your loved one may be confused.

Many people feel hostile when confronted.

Gently try to express your concerns to your loved one.

Take care not to be confrontational or threatening.

46 | *your responsibility. I have to tell you that our supervisor has noticed and they're talking about your poor work."*

"Do you mean to tell me that my job is at risk?" asks Janice, more worried than before.

"I can't speak for the boss, but I know he's frustrated with your performance," answers Jeannie.

Notice how Jeannie presents her story with words like "I feel," "I had to," and "I have to tell you," instead of just saying "you did this" and "you did that." This way Jeannie doesn't have to attack Janice, and it is more difficult for Janice to disagree with Jeannie's personal feelings. This speech also does Janice a big favor by giving her information about the new situation at work: Her job is at risk.

Harriet says, "Mom, we need you to help us. I don't like it when you aren't home. Please stay home and be with us. When will you get better? Can we go out and get dinner when you feel good?"

Finally, Carla speaks. "Janice, you're my baby sister and I know you better than anyone else. I know all of your great qualities, like your charm and your great sense of humor. Remember all the pranks we used to play on Dad? You and I both got married and now we both have beautiful, intelligent children. You're a tough woman and you're making it, but now, just barely. Your family is in trouble because of the drinking and the pills."

"I had no idea that this was happening. Why didn't anyone say something sooner?" asks Janice as she puts her head between her knees.

Harriet speaks in her own words instead of saying something that an adult relative or counselor told her to say. Her speech is simple and direct. Carla finishes her speech, and then tells Janice that they are ready to take her to an inpatient treatment program. All she has to do is agree to get better. Janice doesn't want to go at first. She asks, "Who will watch my kids?" and "What about my job?" But the group is ready. Carla and Jorge will have no problem keeping a close watch on Jay and Harriet, and the office where Janice and Jeannie work has agreed to give Janice the time off if she agrees to do all the hard work necessary to successfully complete the addiction treatment program.

Because the group rehearsed several times, they were able to anticipate Janice's objections. That afternoon Jorge and Carla drive Janice to the center for treatment.

48 *Things to Remember About Intervention Day*

Organizing and leading an intervention is a very demanding task. Usually an adult who is not a member of the immediate family will lead the intervention.

Although you may not be the leader of an intervention group, you can help out the leader. Keep in mind that:

- Everyone should write down notes and even complete speeches before the intervention. Do not forget your notes on intervention day. You may be a little nervous and the notes will guide you.

- Each person should stick to his own story. Use phrases that begin with "I," such as "I noticed that" and "I felt like."

- Let the group leader control the speaking order and the amount of time each person speaks. Let the group leader handle questions that the addicted loved one might ask, and let the leader speak directly to anyone in the group who becomes angry or upset.

Questions That Will Remain Unanswered for Now

Not all interventions go as smoothly as the one you have just witnessed. In fact, no two interventions are alike. Many will not end with a resolution of the problem. But each group should formulate a goal for the meeting, such as getting the addicted loved one to agree to enroll in a treatment program.

Sometimes the loved one will not agree to do this. That is okay. The group has let him or her know that they are aware of the problem and they're ready to help. The members of the group have also learned about changing their behaviors to stop enabling their loved one. The time has come to allow the addicted loved one to face the negative consequences of his or her addiction.

If the group members agree to practice tough love, they will no longer cover up for their loved one. For example, Jeannie might not purchase the missing supplies with her own money if she is using tough love. Jeannie might let Janice face her angry supervisor, even if Janice might lose her job as a result. As you can imagine, practicing tough love is not easy. There are many reasons why a friend would cover for her

50 | addicted coworker. After the intervention, you know that everyone involved is going to stop covering up.

If your loved one agrees to enter a treatment program, the prognosis is good. But even with this result your loved one must still undergo a sometimes long and painful recovery. Remember, the addiction is a serious illness. If your loved one refuses treatment, there is still hope. Your intervention has planted a seed. This is the idea that recovery is an option. The group members should stand by this idea, and consider that sometimes a second, or even a third, intervention can bring better results.

CHAPTER 4

What Does the Future Hold?

For the first time, someone has spoken up. Maybe you have told your best friend how she hurts you when she drinks too much. Or maybe you have just begun to see the changes in your family members now that you have begun to plan your intervention. You will find that others around you can tell the same kinds of stories you can. If you attend meetings for family members of alcoholics, such as Alateen, you meet others who have the same kinds of stories that you have. At every level and for everyone involved, intervention helps to break down the denial and enabling that go on when silence prevails.

The process of healing continues long after the intervention.

After the intervention, Jay felt better than he had for many months. Just learning about his mom's addiction was helpful, but speaking about the problems it caused him was even better. Now he knows that he was not to blame and that the other members of his family will not continue to act as if nothing is the matter. He was nervous about the day his mom would come home from the treatment center. Will he have to practice tough love?

The Addicted Person

Remember that your intervention will help no matter what happens in the end. Presenting the facts to your loved one will help that person know that he or she has hurt you and also that there is still hope for

recovery. Your addicted loved one might 53
agree to enter treatment or attend a twelve-
step program. But on the other hand, he or
she might not. This person has lived with
the attitude that "nothing is wrong" for
some time now. This denial is one of the
biggest obstacles to overcome. If your
group can demonstrate facts that the addicted loved one knows to be true, then you
will have gone a long way toward overcoming denial. If your addicted loved one
accepts the offer of treatment, then you
have come even closer to your goal of
helping your loved one begin the recovery
process. At the very least, your intervention
informs your loved one that life as he or she
knows it is about to change for good.

Your Family and the Intervention Group

Even if your one-on-one or group intervention does not succeed in making a major
change in your loved one's behavior, you
have succeeded in reaching out and opening
the lines of communication. You have more
options, too. You may seek professional help,
such as counseling, now that you have experienced how good communicating can make
you feel. If you tried a simple intervention
that didn't work, you may think about how
to start a group intervention yourself. Many

54 young people have successfully initiated group interventions themselves by contacting a counselor.

Sometimes family members live far away, but they still want to participate. Even though they may not be able to attend all of the meetings, this is still possible. Some counselors can arrange to have relatives in distant cities or states go through their own counseling sessions. Sessions can be videotaped and mailed to these group members so that they can hear what everyone has to say before the intervention. Just because a family is spread out across the country does not mean that they cannot come together to perform an intervention. Everyone must still commit to preparation, but the whole process can bring everyone closer together.

As you read in the first chapter, you and your family members fell into a routine before anyone came up with the idea of intervening. In this routine, you all lived in fear that your addicted loved one might get worse, but no one did anything about it. Maybe you all were afraid that trying to help might fail, or might even create a worse situation than before. This caused hopelessness, anger, and a lot of depression. Because the intervention process teaches you all about addiction and about the chances of recovery, your hopelessness, anger, and depression will subside.

What Has Changed for Good

As you begin to prepare for your group's intervention, you may begin to notice some changes around you. The people on the team might begin to live with some hope. Each person will begin to let go of his enabling the addicted loved one. Just talking about the ways you have been hurt will help you. After the intervention, you should continue this process of healing yourself. A support group might be the best way to keep on talking after the intervention is over. Some possibilities are professionals who work with groups like Alateen and Al-Anon; religious or youth-group leaders; and teachers, coaches, or other trusted friends. Maintaining this kind of support will help you as your loved one goes through the difficult recovery process.

Janice looked angry as she got into the car with Carla and Jorge on her way to an inpatient treatment program. Jay noticed the expression on his mom's face. "I'm glad she's going. That's what we all wanted. But what will they do to her? Will it hurt?"

56

Jay feels alone, and his younger sister, Harriet, feels confused. She wonders if Mom might need to rely on them more now that she's going to get better. But both of Janice's children will come to be glad that Janice agreed to take such a bold step.

If you've been through an intervention, then you know what the first days are like afterward. It's not easy. Your loved one might promise to quit, only to relapse, or fall back into addiction after only a short time. If your loved one went into rehabilitation, then most likely you were not allowed to visit for many days. But you also might have sensed that everything has changed. Whether or not your intervention changed the behavior of your addicted loved one, some things did change for good.

First, you and the other participants of the intervention have changed your behavior. You will no longer have to sit in painful, silent acceptance of your loved one's addiction. Second, your loved one can never again make excuses without remembering what was said on intervention day. Your loved one knows that you are all very aware of his problem.

The worst part about living with someone who is addicted is sitting by silently

and watching that person become ill be- |
cause you don't know how to communicate. Use intervention to tell the person
that you care, to show that help is on the
way, and most of all, to show that everything has changed for the better. Now you
know what intervention is. If you think you
know someone who might benefit from this
kind of experience, get help to organize an
intervention as soon as you can.

Glossary

addiction The physical or psychological need to use a chemical substance again and again.

blackout A period of time during which an addict can function but has no memory of the time afterward.

codependency The behavior of family or friends that allows an addicted person to continue to use drugs. Family members become codependent because they are afraid to hurt or anger their addicted loved one.

conditioned behaviors Learned actions that a person uses in order to cope with, or get by, during difficult situations.

crisis A sudden, unforeseen problem that causes great pain to an addict and his family. Sometimes a crisis makes an addict realize that treatment is necessary.

denial Pretending that nothing is wrong, even in the face of facts that say otherwise. One of the symptoms of addiction.

enable   To help an addict to continue to use a chemical substance by protecting him from the negative consequences of his actions.

group intervention   An organized meeting including a leader, a counselor, several family members, coworkers, and friends who attempt to force an addicted loved one to accept the reality of his illness, as well as the responsibility of beginning treatment.

intervention   Stepping in and putting a stop to something. In terms of drug addiction, it is making an addicted person face reality.

one-on-one intervention   A meeting between one person and his or her addicted loved one during which the person tries to confront the loved one about his or her addiction.

relapse   When a drug user returns to drug use after a period of not using drugs.

role-playing   During a training session, when a counselor pretends to be the addicted loved one while family members talk about situations that hurt or embarrassed them.

tolerant   Able to accept a certain amount of a drug without feeling its effects.

tough love   The practice of letting an addicted loved one face the consequences of his or her negative actions.

Where to Go for Help

In the United States
Al-Anon/Alateen Family Group Headquarters
1600 Corporate Landing Parkway
Virginia Beach, VA 23454-5617
(800) 344-2666

Alcoholics Anonymous
468 Park Avenue South
New York, NY 10016
(212) 870-3400

Children of Alcoholics Foundation, Inc.
Box 4185, Grand Central Station
New York, NY 10115
(800) 359-COAF

CoAnon Family Groups
P.O. Box 64742-66
Los Angeles, CA 90064
(310) 859-2206

Hazelden Foundation
P.O. Box 11
Center City, MN 55012-0011
(800) 257-7800

Nar-Anon Family Groups
P.O. Box 2562
Palos Verdes Peninsula, CA 90274
(310) 547-5800

National Clearinghouse for Alcohol and Drug
    Information
P.O. Box 2345
Rockville, MD 20847-2345
(800) 729-6686

National Council on Alcoholism and Drug
    Dependence (NCADD)
12 West 21st Street
New York, NY 10010
(800) NCA-CALL

National Institute on Drug Abuse
(800) 662-HELP

In Canada
Addictions Foundation of Manitoba
1031 Portage Avenue
Winnepeg, MB R3G 0R8
(204) 944-6200

Narcotics Anonymous
P.O. Box 7500, Station A
Toronto, ON M5W 1P9
(416) 691-9519

Web Sites
Al-Anon and Alateen
http://www.Al-Anon-Alateen.org

Alcoholics Anonymous Meeting Database
http://www.easydoesit.org

Cocaine Anonymous
http://www.ca.org

Narcotics Anonymous
http://www.wsoinc.com

For Further Reading

Hafen, Brent Q., and Brenda Peterson. *The Crisis Intervention Handbook.* Englewood Cliffs, NJ: Prentice Hall, 1982.

Johnson, Vernon E. *Intervention: How to Help Someone Who Doesn't Want Help.* Minneapolis, MN: Johnson Institute, 1986.

O'Neill, J., and P. O'Neill. *Concerned Intervention: When Your Loved One Won't Quit Alcohol or Drugs.* Oakland, CA: New Harbinger Publications, Inc., 1992.

White, Robert K., and Deborah George Wright. *Addiction Intervention.* New York: Haworth Press, 1998.

Videos

Hazelden Foundation
Structured Intervention; Back to Reality; and *The Invisible Line.*
Call (800) 421-4609 to order.

Johnson Institute
The Intervention; Choices and Consequences; and *Intervention.*
Call (800) 321-5165 to order.

Index

63

About the Author

Craig Konieczko founded his own English as a Second Language program, called A.B.L.E., for immigrants to Brooklyn, New York, where he also lives. He grew up in Maine.

Photo Credits

Cover photo and p. 28 by Ira Fox; p. 12 by Brian Silak; all other photos by Bob Van Lindt.

Design and Layout

Laura Murawski and Michael Caroleo